The Life of John Wesley

The Life of

An Account in Verse

C. Edward Blackburn

Providence House Publishers
PROVIDENCE PUBLISHING CORPORATION
FRANKLIN, TENNESSEE

Printed in the United States of America

| 07 | 06 | 05 | 04 | 03 | 1 | 2 | 3 | 4 | 5 |

Library of Congress Catalog Card Number: 2002117587

ISBN: 1-57736-299-3

Cover design by Gary Bozeman

PROVIDENCE HOUSE PUBLISHERS
an imprint of
Providence Publishing Corporation
238 Seaboard Lane • Franklin, Tennessee 37067
www.providencepubcorp.com
800-321-5692

TO MY WIFE
Emily
and

TO OUR FOUR CHILDREN
*Paul, Winnie, Charlie,
and Clay*

My loves, my inspirations,
and my friends.

Contents

Foreword

RECENT YEARS HAVE MULTIPLIED the attempts to describe and appropriate the remarkable life and legacy of John Wesley. But how does one capture the essence of a man who preached some fifty thousand sermons, kept a detailed journal and diary during most of his eighty-eight years, authored volumes of letters and tracts, and wrote Bible commentaries and theological treatises? How can a movement that spans three hundred years be described briefly in a form accessible to the masses?

Methodism has given birth to numerous scholars, a growing number of whom now specialize in "Wesley studies." Wesley scholars are contributing immeasurably to the wealth of information about the Wesleys and the revival they sparked in the eighteenth century which continues into the twenty-first century.

John Wesley, however, was primarily a preacher and a "practical theologian" whose main concern was the formation of disciples of Jesus Christ. His interest went far beyond intellectual discourse regarding the Christian faith. He was an evangelist of God's grace incarnate in Jesus Christ, and he sought to make that grace real in ordinary people's lives. Wesley gathered people into class meetings and societies where they learned the tenets of the faith and engaged in practices that enabled them to grow in their love for God and neighbor.

Poetry is a major component of the Wesleyan revival. Some scholars have suggested that the Methodist movement is understood best through the poetry and hymns of the Wesleys. Indeed, Wesleyan theology is a sung theology and has been most effectively passed from generation to generation through hymns.

It is appropriate, then, that poetry be employed as a medium for telling the story of Methodism's origins. This unique volume captures in verse the heart of the Methodist heritage. Through the economy of words possible only through poetry, a creative preacher succeeds in providing an accessible and memorable summary of the rich heritage of "the people called Methodist."

Kenneth L. Carder
Bishop, Mississippi Area
The United Methodist Church

Preface and Acknowledgments

THE LIFE OF JOHN WESLEY has been viewed from many angles—historical, theological, sociological, psychological, and in a combination of two or more of these. Some books have been written specifically for children or youth, and others for adults. A few have included pictures to help tell the story. One thing that is common to all of these books is that they have been written in prose.

A few years ago, I decided to write about the life of Wesley in verse. This decision came after a lengthy period of writing hymns and other verse. It also came after spending three summers in England preaching, reading, and visiting places prominent in Wesley's life.

It is my feeling that in a few lines poetry can tell a story concisely and convincingly, while enhancing the feelings involved. This has been especially evident to me in the hymns of Charles Wesley. In a few beautiful words, he captured and presented the Wesleyan theology which has blessed—and continues to bless—millions around the world.

I share these verses with you in appreciation of John Wesley as the chief leader of the Methodist movement. I also present them in recognition of Samuel and Charles Wesley, his father and brother, as writers of verse.

If these verses help the reader to catch the mood and spirit of John Wesley and the early Methodists, or if they cause anyone to be a better member of our Lord's church, I will have been rewarded tenfold.

I am grateful to the following persons who read the manuscript and whose suggestions were most helpful: Joe Hale, David Eliason, Fred Cloud, Frank Gulley, Bishop Kenneth Carder, Eddie Fox, Jim Roy, and Andrew Miller.

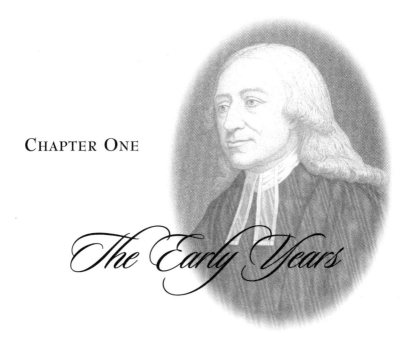

CHAPTER ONE

The Early Years

INTRODUCTION

A great awakening was due
For English towns and dales.
God was preparing His leader;
His planning never fails.

Quietly He groomed John Wesley
To move across the land
With challenging Good News for all;
On him God laid His hand.

EPWORTH

The long grooming process began
At the old Epworth Manse,
Where God through parents did so much
His Christian life to enhance.

Susanna, his devout mother,
Was his early guiding light;
Through her, God helped him get ready
For leadership not in sight.

Susanna was devout and firm—
Good manners were a must;
As she taught each of her children,
She earned their daily trust.

She taught John to read the Scriptures,
Organize his life, and pray;
All of these chores and much, much more
Would help in a future day.

God rescued John when he was six
As the Old Manse burned to the ground;
No one ever let him forget;
He knew it was profound.

A brand snatched from the burning fire—
He had a destiny.
Somewhere along his long life span
He would God's preacher be.

But little did he know that night
What was in store for him—
He only knew that all were safe,
And he thanked God with them.

The people there rebuilt the Manse
Much better than before;
Such love and generosity
No Wesley could ignore.

The Wesleys worked and prayed each day
And lived the Christian life;
They were examples to the town
Of how to live in strife.

He learned to value scholarship
From his own father priest;
In all his academic work,
This was for him the yeast.

John knew his region's history—
Of it he was not proud.

It was known for its poverty,
And life was in a shroud.

Forest and waste land once prevailed,
And much was known as marsh;
But even when these lands were drained,
Life still was very harsh.

In northern Lincolnshire,
A hotbed of unrest,
Politics was a major theme
For good, better, or best.

Even Susanna and Samuel
Differed in politics;
This, at one time, made Samuel leave
Since he couldn't stand the pricks.

Wesley was very much aware
Of tensions in his time;
He was aware of poverty
And its related crime.

Wesley's father had a garden
To try to make ends meet;
But even with what it produced,
His debts he couldn't delete.

Samuel was Epworth's only priest,
And was by some despised;
But it was here that his children
Were nurtured and baptized.

Two sons became ordained young priests,
And this delighted him;
They were well-trained at home and schools
When times were poor and grim.

Both John and Charles became well-known—
A hymnist Charles became;
And John, a priest evangelist—
They blessed the Wesley name.

When John couldn't preach in his home church,
He preached on Samuel's grave,
And people came outside the church
To hear this hometown knave.

He also preached at the town cross,
And many came to hear;
They liked the way he shared Good News;
He made it very clear.

CHARTER HOUSE

Small Charter House, a school for boys,
Became John's home at ten.
It was a tower of learning
As tall as old Big Ben.

His older brother Samuel
Was there when he arrived;
And with his help he settled down,
Adjusted, and survived.

4

In this small school away from home
And at so young an age,
He learned to discipline himself
And learned the printed page.

And it was here that disciplines
Of study and exercise
Formed a pattern that would help him
To be healthy and wise.

OXFORD

He went from Charter House to Oxford,
Where priests are taught and trained.
His academic work fulfilled,
As teacher he remained.

Oxford was a town of towers
And also one of spires;
And its great university
Is one the world admires.

While there he learned Hebrew and Greek
And much theology;
While these were ground on which to stand,
Prayer was his canopy.

Wesley cherished his teaching role
All the years he was there;
They showed a life of discipline—
A must in spirit's care.

Together John and Charles read books
During their Oxford days;
They read aloud and gave their views
And shared in other ways.

During these conditioning years
At the school of their choice,
John joined his brother's Holy Club
And soon was its strong voice.

He couldn't forget the Holy Club,
Of which he was a part.
It disciplined his Christian faith
And fed his longing heart.

5

This Oxford club of many friends
He chaired by their consent;
Not a moment did he regret
The time with them he spent.

George Whitefield and John's brother Charles
Were members of this club;
And in his long and fruitful life,
They were his friendship hub.

Of all he was the only priest,
The one who had the drive
To discipline this holy group
And make it come alive.

Weekly they shared the Eucharist
In humbleness and prayer

And took an offering for the poor
To whom they went with care.

The group was called Enthusiasts
And Holy Club by some;
And others called them Bible moths,
Or something that was dumb.

Of all the names that they were called
By students and the rest,
The one that stuck was Methodists,
Since it described them best.

They had a method in their ways
Which was to them profound;
In their devotion to their Lord,
These Methodists were bound.

They read the Scriptures every week
And prayed that God would rule
In every part of daily life
And even in their school.

This was their method and their plan
On which they did insist—
Observing closely, students teased
And called them Methodists.

To them it was a compliment,
But it wasn't meant that way;
Because of their chosen disciplines,
It was the name to stay.

In their slothful and wicked age
Filled with all kinds of crime,
They met, worshiped, and did good deeds
At a specific time.

They shared their faith with prisoners
And visited the poor;
By being like the early church,
They felt their hearts were pure.

In Christ they trusted for their strength;
In Scripture for insight;
And for the will to follow Christ,
They prayed both day and night.

MISSIONARY TO GEORGIA
Few sermons did he ever preach
Prior to his Georgia stay;
He went to save the Indians there
Returning in dismay.

Something was lacking in his soul—
But what, he was not sure—
Until Moravians helped him
On his long outward tour.

Moravians were blessing him
In simple ways of grace;
He felt it on the stormy sea
When they were face-to-face.

When faced with dangers of the sea,
This group had little fear;
John could not say this for himself,
But wished to feel God near.

This long trip to America
To share with Indians there
Left him with many doubts—
Since their response was rare.

He even had some trouble with
The colonists as well;
His strictness as preacher and priest
Pushed him into his shell.

His disappointments sent him home
Not knowing what to do;
With doubts still stirring in his soul,
What should he now pursue?

Arriving back in London town,
He met with some dear friends,
Told them of these predicaments,
Which seemed to have no ends.

They were the ones who understood
His problems from the start;
They knew that Christ was in his head,
But was Christ in his heart?

They calmly but surely advised
That he spend time in prayer,
Preach faith until it's in the heart,
Then preach because it's there.

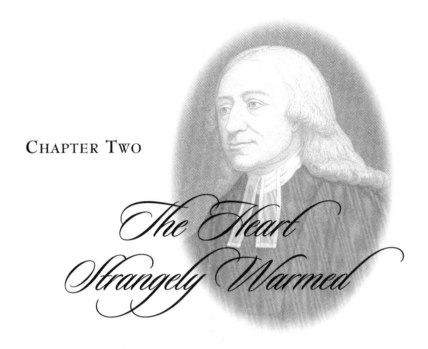

CHAPTER TWO

The Heart Strangely Warmed

The seeker and the sought was John
In those early years;
He was faithful in seeking Christ,
But often filled with fears.

God was reaching out to his soul
And touching it sometime.
He slowed him down at Aldersgate
And touched his soul sublime.

John Wesley's heart was strangely warmed
When he felt Christ's loving care
In a little weekly meeting
Where some had met for prayer.

While Luther's preface to Paul's words
To the Christians at Rome
Was being read, something happened—
Wesley's heart felt *shalom*.

Within his heart of hearts, he knew
That Christ had saved his soul;
Even his sin was forgiven—
His life was now a whole.

The joy he felt he couldn't contain—
To Charles he ran to share;
Charles welcomed John and his good news;
He, too, had news to bear.

Charles told his brother John that night
That Christ had come to him;
And his heart, too, was strangely warmed—
God had blessed both of them.

Assurance was the gift God gave,
And this they never lost;
It helped lead them to share the Christ
And never count the cost.

These heartwarming experiences
Were vital to each soul;
They were given and heart-felt
And made their lives a whole.

They shared a common ministry
But in a different way;
John preached and Charles put into hymns
What they wanted to say.

The awesome doctrines of God's grace
Were stated in the hymns;
And to the growing Methodists
Were common as the Thames.

After his Aldersgate event,
John had some searching days;
He sought out the Moravians—
He had to learn their ways.

He took a trip to Germany
Where Zinzendorf he met;

For what he learned from all of them,
He knew he owed a debt.

He spent many days at Herrnhut
With open mind and heart;
He learned their methods and their ways
Of which he was a part.

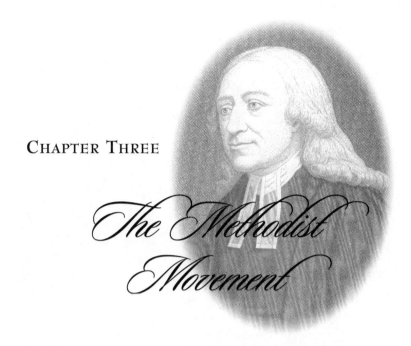

CHAPTER THREE

The Methodist Movement

CONDITIONS OF HIS TIME (1703–1791)

> His age was known for its coarseness
> And inequalities;
> Hangings were common in his days
> And so were paupers' pleas.
>
> Over one-half of children died
> Before the age of five;
> He lived in difficult rare times
> In which to stay alive.
>
> Disease, workhouse, and curse of gin
> Depressed the people's goals;
> But Wesley came with God's Good News,
> Which would save sinners' souls.
>
> Only a few people could read,
> And fewer folk could write;
> Assaults were common in the streets,
> And hunger was a blight.

Retreating morals and beliefs
Were taking their great toll;
Yet they helped him to clarify
His own God-given role.

Locked into mediocrity
In almost every mind,
England was suffering turmoil
Of the religious kind.

The church had turned its thoughts inward
While the poor tried to cope;
Being satisfied with itself,
The church gave little hope.

In an age when the church was dull
And often out of touch,
It gave the people little help
When they were needing much.

Schisms and controversies
And heresies within
Weakened the life of the state church
And helped the people sin.

Wesley was a much-needed balm
To soothe a troubled mind;
The times were hard, poverty reigned,
Most folks were in a bind.

Speaking against complacency
Was not the thing to do;
So when Wesley challenged the church,
He was one of a few.

He did attack man's wickedness
And man's moral decay;
He shared the Christ through his talents,
All for a better day.

With his high principles and zeal
And strong Christian background,

His message to the church and world
Was nothing but profound.

Attacking wickedness in church
And in society,
Leaders in both responded fast;
All felt the rivalry.

Many pulpits were closed to him
By priests who were in charge;
The loss to them and to their towns
In retrospect was large.

Opposition was no stranger
In most places he went;
While sharing biblical Good News,
He asked folks to repent.

Most of his oppositions came
Soon after Aldersgate
When heartwarmed preaching and outreach
Began to dominate.

14

In towns like Wednesbury and Walsall,
He faced an angry mob;
But as a pioneer for Christ
This was part of his job.

With confidence he faced the mobs
And frankly shared with them;
When they saw his sincerity,
Many respected him.

England was puzzled by this man—
Yes, he was young but bright;
He was the bright and shining star
In England's darkest night.

He had a passion for all souls
And sought to win each one;
To this great task he set his face
Until his life was done.

Neglected masses he embraced
With Christ-like love and care;
He went to them and shared with them.
They felt his presence there.

His deeds did shine in darkened times
Like stars in heaven's dome,
And they like them when really seen,
Pointed the wayward home.

Many thousand were won to Christ
Through his true faithfulness;
His life pointed the way to Christ
And took away the guess.

In his eighty-eight years of life,
He rode, he walked, he stood
For Christ and all that Christ had taught,
Doing all that he could.

15

"You've nothing to do but to save souls"—
This was a Wesley rule;
"Therefore, spend and be spent," he taught,
By using every tool.

Charles Wesley put into his hymns
What John in sermons shared;
They had a common Christian faith
Which they with joy declared.

Sweet singer of Methodism
He was so often called,
But had there been a prince of hymns,
Charles would have been installed.

He had a strong desire to serve
The Christ who died for him
And wrote his many Christian hymns
To share with all of them.

The Wesley brothers preached and sang
Religion of the heart
And worked it out in daily deeds—
This was a Christian art.

They knew that they were called of God—
A charge to keep they had;
The message of God's love they shared
With each adult and lad.

And by the thousands people came
To hear these men of God;
Their souls were saved in rented halls
And sitting on the sod.

These newborn Christian souls were taught
To study God's own way
As found in Scripture, old and new,
And follow it each day.

PREACHING AND GROWING REVIVAL
Preaching was part of ministry—
The largest part for him;
Of all the preachers of his day,
He was well-known to them.

He said, "The world is my parish,"
And went where he was led;
All places were sacred to him;
He preached with heart and head.

His sermons were optimistic
And Godly in content;
They were lengthy but to the point,
And many thought God-sent.

Attacked by church authorities
And from their pulpits barred,
He preached in houses and in fields;
His gospel was not marred.

The centers of revivals were
In cities Wesley knew.
In London and in Bristol town
He had much work to do.

Often he traveled to each place
This holy work to share.
Nothing about the revivals
Escaped his tender care.

Many people were converted
As Wesley preached God's Word;
And many of them were faithful
Obeying what they heard.

Societies were formed to help
Them grow and to obey
The rudiments of Christian faith
And follow in Christ's way.

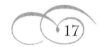

It was Whitefield who got Wesley
To preach in open air,
In Bristol first and London next,
When such preaching was rare.

The preaching in the open field
Was questioned by him at first;
But after giving it a try,
He felt it not accursed.

George Whitefield had won him over
And knew that he was right;
Wesley learned to do good preaching
With no building in sight.

The world has its stately buildings;
The world has open field;
The purpose of his preaching
Was helping sinners yield.

The miners came to hear him speak
Under the roof of sky;
They heard his message in the fields
And knew that God was nigh.

When Methodist small groups had grown
And spread over the land,
God convinced him that lay preaching
Could be a helping hand.

Thomas Maxwell, first lay preacher,
Did not Wesley obey;
He had been preaching at the Foundry
While John had been away.

John was angry with him at first—
His mother calmed him down
With glowing praises for Maxwell
And a tug on John's gown.

"Do not judge him 'til he is heard,"
She said in her kind way;
John Wesley heard what she told him
And selected a day.

From what he heard and what he saw,
His heart was slowly changed;
And before many months had passed,
Lay preaching was arranged.

Reluctantly receiving them,
He kept a firm control
And taught them how to preach God's Word
And feed a hungry soul.

Accepting field and lay preaching,
He proved he could adjust;

Whatever moved the church forward,
In it he put his trust.

Sufficient, sovereign, saving grace
Was what John Wesley preached;
And with the message of God's love
Thousands of souls he reached.

OUTREACH AND MINISTRY
His whole incredible career
Reflected noble trust
In Christ his Lord, who guided him
In doing what he must.

Early before the light of day
He read and prayed God's Word.
To do something other than this
It never once occurred.

During this time while others slept
He prayed God's will be done
And rising from this time of prayer
He acted as God's son.

19

This discipline gave him insight,
Kept him close to his Source,
And strengthened his ability
To preach God's Word with force.

All through the day he would look back
And know from whence help came.
This anchored him in his bold faith
And kept his life the same.

This morning watch—this time with God—
Was his own master key
Which did unlock his soul and mind
To God's eternity.

Jeremy Taylor's own deep thoughts
Nourished his hungry soul

And the ideals of William Law
Helped make his life a whole.

He knew the Greek New Testament
As a good scholar should—
And shared his knowledge faithfully
As a good preacher could.

God's Holy Word was his compass
And daily prayer his chart;
He preached his way across the land
And shared with them his heart.

He praised his Maker while he breathed—
A part of holiness—
And served his Maker joyfully—
From this he wouldn't digress.

His grace-filled love nourished his flock—
Preacher and lay alike—
He knew the time to pamper them
And also when to strike.

A champion for the poor and weak,
He gave to them his best;
And loving them with heart and mind,
He gave to them the rest.

The poor and disenchanted folk
Found hope in what he said;
They sensed his messages were real.
To Christ many were led.

He helped them keep their dignity
Through the gospel he preached;
And for the kingdom of his God,
Many of them were reached.

They found in him a friend in deed
And in his message hope.
He helped them see the light of Christ,
And Christ helped them to cope.

He saw the sick and knew that they
Had little doctor care;
He was concerned in their good health
And wrote a book to share.

He wrote about home remedies
Which all could understand
And set up dispensaries
To lend a helping hand.

Total persons were his concern—
The body, mind, and soul.
He lived his life to help others
And make their lives a whole.

He lived the eighteenth century
And was part of it all;
He knew people in all walks of life
From government to stall.

Horses were a part of his life
Across his many years.
He chose this means of traveling
As did his many peers.

The horses were dependable
And were convenient, too;
Without them he was limited
As to what he could do.

Two-hundred-fifty thousand miles
By horse and thousands reached;
And forty-two thousand sermons
In a lifetime he preached.

He was the horseman of the Lord—
Proclaimer of Good News.
He traveled far and faced hardships;
In all he paid his dues.

John Wesley had helpers for sure
And they were not a few.

The greatest was his brother Charles
With him the movement grew.

Between the brothers, Charles and John,
There was an earthly bond,
And in their common faith in Christ
Their love went far beyond.

Their disagreements, which were few,
Were not to be compared
With all the blessings God gave them
Which they together shared.

Their joys and disappointments too
On all the British Isles
Are found within John's *Diary*
And other written files.

Charles had the mind of an artist
And John a scholar's mind—
Yet in their sharing ministry
Each one of these we find.

Charles was more enthusiastic.
John had a calmer zeal.
In everything they said and did
Their love for Christ was real.

In his long fruitful ministry
A hymnist Charles became,
Writing thousands of Christian hymns
Which later brought him fame.

Although John wrote just a few hymns,
He edited hymn books;
These were needed for his movement
As much as sheep need brooks.

The movement grew by leaps and bounds—
God's spirit gave success;
Across England God's Spirit led
Despite the English press.

John was the head and Charles, the heart—
Yet both shared mind and heart;
John blended statesmanship and grace;
With hymns Charles did his part.

The "Sweet Singer of Israel"
Was faithful to the end.
He put in hymns the Scripture thoughts
From this he would not bend.

By taking tunes the people knew,
Charles helped them sing Good News,
Which he had shaped with his own words,
Reflecting Wesley views.

Theology expressed in hymns—
And sung with great delight—
Gave strength to the Wesley movement
And made its future bright.

The basic doctrines in God's Word
Through Charles were simplified;
And his influence on the movement
Will never be denied.

23

Enthusiasm was bad taste
In religion for sure,
But in the Wesley revivals,
Excitement would endure.

More than a few were known to shout—
Singing was lively, too;
The preaching was inspired and strong,
and the conversions grew.

John Wesley was a pragmatist—
This all movements require;
Some changes he could tolerate
Against his own desire.

Lay preaching was just one of these;
He had to turn to it.

As more societies were formed
He knew he must submit.

No one in his century
Was better known than he;
People of every class and clan
Had felt his charity.

Wesley interpreted God's Word,
And made God's plan so clear;
The common folk loved him for this
And followed without fear.

He organized societies
To help the Christians grow.
In doing this he faced hardships
And every kind of woe.

John knew that he must be in charge
And closely supervise.
The progress of societies
Revealed that he was wise.

Lay preachers and class leaders, too,
Absorbed much of his time,
But this was time well-spent for him
And some did call it prime.

He helped them understand his rules
And his theology.
He strongly emphasized to them
Accountability.

The Methodist mission abroad
In the new continent
Was to spread scriptural holiness.
This was Wesley's intent.

He sent friends, Asbury and Coke,
To the new colonies
To oversee the movement there
And all its ministries.

He was well-pleased as time went by
To see the movement grow.
He knew a harvest always comes
To those who plan and sow.

Though he was little in stature,
He stood tall in God's sight—
Being faithful in every day
And loyal every night.

What Wesley started in his day
Under his Lord's command
Goes on today around the world
In almost every land.

We know our roots (and they are deep)
Go back to Wesley's day,
But power of the Methodists
Is Christ; He's here to stay.

That's why United Methodists
For centuries to come
Will be around to serve their Lord;
Nothing can keep them mum.

Preaching and varied ministries
Will lift the Christ up high
And point the way for struggling souls;
On Christ they can rely.

He left those who refused God's love
In God's eternal hands;
God led him on to preach Good News
To help with His commands.

With all his limitations known,
His life and ministry
Still magnify and point to God
Who sets His people free.

He still prods us to be like Christ
In all of our outreach
To focus on needs of the poor
Whether we preach or teach.

WESLEY, THE ORGANIZER
Organization as a gift
From God he had received;
By using it at the right time,
Great things would be achieved.

Societies were formed to help
The followers obey
The rudiments of Christian faith
And love the Christian way.

His very first society,
Which was at Fetter's Lane,
Was supervised closely by him.
Others from it would gain.

For many followers of Christ,
These were a means of grace
Which brought to people in hard times
A bright and happy face.

Ideals from Oxford's Holy Club
In class meetings took hold
And pushed Wesley's movement forward
With spirit rich and bold.

Through class leaders, Wesley controlled
The meetings and their goals
To edify all searching hearts
And sanctify all souls.

He used what he could find at hand—
He had an open view;
John Wesley was the first to know
This system was not new.

How he used it was his genius—
The system worked for him;
Through it he cared for new converts
And strengthened all of them.

The vigils and love feasts he got
From early Christian days
And used them to help Methodists
Improve their Christian ways.

Believing every Christian should
Regularly renew
His holy vow to God and church,
He offered something new.

He started covenant services
In the societies,
And Methodists became stronger
While praying on their knees.

WESLEY, THE WRITER
His *Journal* helped his followers;
Its volumes numbered eight;
Through it his spiritual values
He did communicate.

We learn from his detailed *Journal*
What he could say and do;
And get a sampling of those things
Which he would not pursue.

His *Journal*—a published record
And portrait of his age—
Had a companion *Diary*
With secrets of the sage.

His *Diary* was never meant
To be published, they say;
He wrote it in symbols and codes
And kept it locked away.

It was a secret reflection
Of his own inward soul;
This code was broken recently
And made his life a whole.

The writer Jeremy Taylor,
With stress on what was pure,
Influenced him at an early stage
In piety for sure.

This search started his *Diary*,
In which he penned his thoughts
About his motives and his aims,
About his do's and ought's.

His *Notes on the New Testament*
Were clear, precise, and short;
At God's command, he used this means
To teach and to exhort.

He wrote them for the common man
Because he sensed the need
To make the Scriptures understood
For all who wished to heed.

His preachers were to know these *Notes*
And share what they contained;
All doctrines which differed from them
Were sure to be *disdained*.

The *Arminian Magazine*,
Which came from his own mind,
Contrasted his view of salvation
With Calvinistic kind.

He often took what others said
And shared it as his own;
But all was done in Christ-like love
To make the Savior known.

He sought no honor for himself
In what he said and did;

His life was like an open book,
And not one thing was hid.

Such openness and love for God
Gave his witness appeal
And helped many God's truth to find
And God's presence to feel.

WESLEY, THE TIRELESS WORKER
Two hundred fifty thousand miles
He traveled in his work;
And not one phase of this movement
Did Wesley ever shirk.

To England, Scotland, and Ireland
He went with heart on fire;
By foot, horseback, ferry, and coach,
He never seemed to tire.

He had something to share with all—
Good News which warms the heart;
He traveled onward day-by-day
Compelled to do his part.

For use of time he had his rules
And these he did obey:
Begin and end each day with God—
An hour with God each day.

The use of time must be correct—
This was one of his rules;
He felt if he misused God's time,
He would be damned with fools.

Be diligent in one's calling;
Avoid curiosity;
Forsake all types of idleness;
Act out theology.

He knew beyond a single doubt
That it would be a crime
To seek one's sanctification
Without good use of time.

His heart-warming simplicity,
His choice of style and word
Conveyed to simple humble folk
What once had gone unheard.

God's spirit was directing him
In what he had to say
To add new souls to our Lord's church
In almost every day.

The movement grew and so did John
In knowledge of God's ways;
He even knew what he must do
To handle all the strays.

Retreat was but a word to him;
His actions proved him right;
There was an inner voice in him
Which gave to him insight.

Mistakes he made: this we can see,
But misdirections, no.
His course was charted by our Lord
To face both friend and foe.

John preached God's Word as he knew it;
He knew it very well—
He emphasized heaven's blessings
And the evils of hell.

In an evil society,
John gave his listeners hope;
He preached the gospel of our Lord
That helped the people cope.

His messages were biblical
And well-applied to life;
He helped folk see their need for God
To deal with all their strife.

By calling folks to confession,
Knowing their sins were great,
He asked them to return to Christ
Before it was too late.

This sense of urgency was felt
In places where he preached;
Through his untiring ministry,
Thousands of souls were reached.

He was an instrument of God
Through which God shared his love;
And all of those who heard him preach
Sensed power from above.

There was not much he did not know
About the Christian way;
He studied Scripture faithfully
And lived his faith each day.

When Wesley preached people listened;
But some did not agree;
On rare occasions where he preached,
He found he had to flee.

Some tried to run him out of town,
But he would hold his ground.
He showed no fear and reasoned well;
His messages were sound.

The faithful listeners who caught
The drift of his own mind
Through what he said and what he wrote
A better life did find.

They listened to the words he spoke
And what he wrote they read;

Their souls were hungry for the truth.
Through Wesley they were fed.

Not so much better as for things,
But better as for peace,
They felt assurance in their souls;
From sin they had release.

Through Wesley God renewed their souls—
They felt newborn within;
Over the evil in their lives,
They knew that they could win.

Mind over matter was his aim—
In this he did succeed;
The things on earth had no appeal—
His aim became his creed.

Wesley was an avid reader
And much he did retain;
He treasured Thomas à Kempis,
Whose joy he tried to gain.

WESLEY, THE REFORMER
Social reform was not Wesley's
Basic concern in life;
It was conversion to the Christ—
This helped with inner strife.

But such reforms were the outgrowth
From inner sacred ground;
He stirred the ground and planted, too;
He knew the work was sound.

A great abuse in Wesley's time
Was that of bribery;
He strongly stressed, "Don't sell your vote,"
Nor stain your honesty.

Against smuggling of every kind
On which many were bent

Wesley wrote *Words to a Smuggler*
And this he put in print.

He asked that prisons be reformed,
Identifying them
As nurseries of wickedness
Which were gross and grim.

Real early in his ministry
He knew philanthropy
Was necessary to help those
Who needed charity.

He also knew that this alone
Was not enough to meet
All needs of those who must have help
To get them off the street.

So he, with one society
And money of his own,
Set up a spinning factory
To use the cotton grown.

Concern about the bad health care
Led him to know for sure
That he must start facilities
In London for the poor.

So in the year of forty-six,
This drive he couldn't resist:
A good physician he did hire
And then a pharmacist.

He was a social reformer
To his very last day—
Always seeking to help the poor
In every kind of way.

From sale of books and pamphlets, too;
A fortune he did make

And gave it all to charity.
The poor he didn't forsake.

Before his time, pity was what
The poor often received;
Wesley maintained they should be helped
And saw that they received.

Seeing children unattended
And children breaking rules
He promoted education
By starting Sunday schools.

During the last years of his life
Many were organized;
Reflecting on this emphasis
His efforts have been prized.

He had strong views on slavery
And called it in research,
"That execrable villainy—,"
A scandal to the church.

In some of the last words he wrote
To William Wilberforce
He backed his fight in Parliament
Against the slavery course.

In his *Thoughts Upon Slavery*,
A strong attack was made.
Concerning this most evil way
His prayers would never fade.

He called American slavedom
"The Vilest ever seen,"
And all of those who held their slaves
Were seen by him as mean.

In seventeen hundred eighty,
According to his views
The American Methodists
Made some earth-shaking news.

In the conference of that year
They took a mighty stand
And declared that all who held slaves
Weren't keeping God's command.

Only six years before this date
Wesley made his decree
That slavery was an evil
In *Thoughts Upon Slavery*.

Although he lived to ripe old age,
He pondered finitude;
Thoughts of his own fragility
His *Journal* did include.

Knowing uncertainty of life,
He took in hand his quill,
And in sound mind and prayerful thought,
He wrote out his own will.

He knew others should do the same
And often told them so;
But few followed his own advice.
It was the status quo.

Confronting evil of his day—
This he could not resist;
Afraid of nothing on this earth,
He was an activist.

In opposition he was made strong
In causes he held dear.
To all authorities he spoke
Without a single fear.

The greatest and lasting reforms
In which he was involved
Were found in hearts of his converts
Who had soul problems solved.

It was through these newborn good souls
Who had a change within,

That helped to change society
Which was so full of sin.

WESLEY, THE THEOLOGIAN

He was a folk theologian
And he was gladly heard;
He brought together faith and works
And lively preached God's Word.

Tradition and experience,
Scripture and reason, too,
Were sources of his strong beliefs
And these he did pursue.

These sources of his Christian faith—
And they are ours today—
Are seen throughout his ministry,
And they didn't go away.

To him Christian faith and works
Must travel hand-in-hand
Based on our sources of belief
And on our Lord's command.

Wesley's balanced theology
Has stood the test of years
And led the people Methodists
And those whom they call peers.

Theology of salvation
Was his major concern
In all his thoughts and words and deeds.
From him much we can learn.

A salvation by faith alone
Is what John Wesley preached,
And with this message of God's love,
Thousands of folks were reached.

Because God first loves His children,
His children can respond;

And this John called prevenient grace;
Of this doctrine he was fond.

Prevenient grace in his own view
Was never something less
Than God's own love within our hearts;
This brings us to confess.

It is our Lord's initiative
Which helps us to respond
To God's redeeming, saving grace,
Which brings about a bond.

He knew we could not all alone
Know God's redeeming grace;
Only initiative from God
Could help him this embrace.

The work of salvation begins
With God's prevenient grace,
And Wesley knew beyond a doubt
This was salvation's base.

37

The entrance to the life of faith
Is through repentance' gate;
And this is something Wesley knew
Could not be left to fate.

The Christian life can't start without
Acknowledgment of sin;
But when we pray, Wesley proclaimed,
New life will then begin.

He knew salvation still requires
Initiative that's shown;
Whereas, prevenient grace is God's—
Repentance is our own.

Free grace, free will—basic beliefs
Through all his ministry—
Were the foundations of his faith—
On this we all agree.

Holy living—holy dying—
Words which describe him best—
Show us a man who lived his faith
And left to God the rest.

The road to Christian holiness
We call the Jesus way;
John Wesley knew this road by heart
And traveled it each day.

Our salvation by faith alone
Must lead to Christian growth—
Inward and outward holiness;
He equally stressed both.

Perfection is not absolute
Nor free from all mistakes;
And it is not infallible
Nor wholeness which one makes.

Christian perfection to Wesley
Was what the word implied—
Process, journey, as well as growth.
On these the word relied.

Perfection is seldom attained—
He knew this in his heart;
Yet it was there in all his goals,
And it would not depart.

Knowing that Christ was the Savior
And that he had been reached,
A holiness of heart and life
Was what John Wesley preached.

John was a Trinitarian—
And this we don't deny;
He got it from God's Holy Word
On which we all rely.

The essence of his faith was found
In the Apostles' Creed;

This simple summary of faith
Backed up his every deed.

He was obsessed with knowing God
And living in God's reign;
The thought of not doing God's will
Brought him much inward pain.

Centrality of ministry
Was with and for the poor
Reflecting his theology
Which would always endure.

Wesley's theology underwrote
All thoughts which he proclaimed;
And where they were not Scripture-based,
They were not where he aimed.

The life of sanctification
Is a good life of prayer;
He knew that it would always be
A life of loving care.

His biblical theology
With Christ as cornerstone
Was the foundation of his work
As history has shown.

Allusions to the Bible came
So naturally to him;
His mind was filled with scriptural thoughts—
Yes, even to the brim.

He leaned his soul against God's Word
And felt his soul secure;
And through the study of the same,
He saw his faith mature.

His thoughts on sin—like those of Paul—
Were positive and sound;
"When sin abounded in this world,
Grace did much more abound."

He had a reasoning sharp mind
And used it prayerfully;
Explaining Christian faith and works
'Til everyone could see.

To him our Christian faith and works
Must travel hand-in-hand
Based on our sources of belief
And on our Lord's command.

In God's image humans were made;
As such they knew no sin;
Holy, complete, and merciful—
Perfect they did begin.

In the stories of Genesis,
Man chose to disobey;
This tendency as strong as then
Is still with us today.

This holy state of perfection
Did not continue long;
Man chose to disobey his God,
And this was something wrong.

But God did not give up on man—
God kept extending grace;
Through prophets, priests, and Jesus Christ,
His love we still can trace.

In essence this is what John preached—
It was what he believed;
With emphasis on Jesus Christ,
His message was received.

In the context of our Lord's church
A Christian's growth takes place

And Wesley was convinced this was
Through different means of grace.

He strongly stressed the sacraments,
Scripture, and preaching, too.
Through these specific means of grace
God does our lives pursue.

WESLEY AND THE SACRAMENTS
The sacraments were dear to him
As were the church's creeds;
He understood each one of them
And how they met man's needs.

With the state church he did agree
On the two sacraments
And wasn't afraid to state the same
In places where he went.

He knew that they were scripture based
And tradition confirmed;
He liked the way the church stressed them
And how each one was termed.

41

Baptism was a mystery
And not merely a sign;
He never had a single doubt
That it was God's design.

It is a means of grace for sure
And was designed for all;
It is for infants and adults,
And it involves a call.

As an initiation rite
Into God's family,
It shows acceptance on God's part
And man's on bended knee.

Baptism was a simple term
Which all could understand;

And it as well as Lord's Supper
Came from the Lord's command.

Baptism in John Wesley's view
Required at least three things;
And these he stressed throughout his life
And benefits each brings.

Ordained priests must perform the rite,
And water must be used
In the name of the Trinity.
On these he wasn't confused.

The Lord's Supper and Baptism
He knew from early days
In Epworth where his father preached.
Through them he knew God's ways.

The Lord's Supper reminded him
That Christ had died for all
To save us from our waywardness
And to God's gracious call.

By kneeling at the altar rail
He felt his humbleness
And taking the two elements
God helped him to confess.

Not once a year or once a month,
But more than once a week,
The Lord's Supper he gladly shared.
This helped him to be meek.

Both sacraments reminded him
Of God's redeeming grace;
In his balanced theology,
Each had its lofty place.

Conclusion

No person in the British Isles
Was better known than he—
Including all the kings and queens
In his own century.

His lofty place in history
To many is well-known;
And his influence on Methodists
Can never be o'er blown.

As founder of the Methodists
Two centuries ago,
He was the noble challenger—
Of the church status quo.

Concerning the established church
Which was barely alive,
John sought never to replace
But only to revive.

John was well-versed in what had passed
And visioned future years;
Aware of what the church should be,
He was ahead of peers.

He was a champion of the poor
Through his strong faith and deed;
He put feet on what was preached—
The poor were helped in need.

In all his many ministries,
His purpose was the same—
To spread God's scriptural holiness
And do it in Christ's name.

He did this by preaching God's Word
In every kind of place—
Inside, outside, small towns, large towns—
He did it through God's grace.

John was a leader from the start—
As seen in Oxford days—
As leader of the Holy Club
In all his Christian ways.

He lived the Scripture every day
And preached it every week;
He knew the Scripture inside out
In Hebrew and in Greek.

Wesley thought in the future tense—
He always planned ahead—
Methodists sprang from noble goals
And followed where he led.

In his eighties he was amazed
At all the strength he had;
He was as strong and as alert
As when he was a lad.

He often prayed in senior years
That he wouldn't useless be;

This prayer was answered and with grace;
He lived life faithfully.

Untiring follower of Christ
From dawn to setting sun—
And father of all Methodists,
He died in ninety-one.

The tireless traveler had come
To his road's end at last;
He felt God's presence in his death
As well as in his past.

John never lost ability
To sense God's presence here.
"The best of all—God is with us,"
He said as death drew near.

Leaving a cherished heritage
With some of it in code,
He died in the presence of friends
At home on City Road.

This code was broken recently,
And he is better known;
The code in his own *Diary*
Revealed how he had grown.

Eighty-eight years he lived on earth—
A life full of God's grace;
His teachings and example, too,
We never can replace.

His biblical theology
With emphasis on grace
Brought hope to hungry, searching souls—
In every needy place.

This same heart-warmed theology
Brings hope to us today.
When it's proclaimed through word and deed
By those who trust and pray.

Epilogue

POEMS BASED ON WESLEY'S LIFE AND FAITH

JOHN WESLEY

Mastermind of Methodists,
Organizer supreme;
No tolerator of schism
And perfector of theme.

A special reed plucked from the fire,
A lover of the church,
Saintly in his cleric attire,
A scholar in research.

A challenger of status quo,
A teacher through his pen,
A volunteer when Christ said, "Go,"
And a fighter of sin.

Disciplinarian by choice,
And a preacher by trade,

For Christ a strong and mighty voice,
For the weary—a shade.

A missionary to the core
With God's compass and chart;
In Methodist structure—the ore,
Evangelist in heart.

EPWORTH
    The two sons of Samuel
    Who were destined to preach
    Were Charles and little John,
    And he was proud of each.

    Epworth was home for John
    Until the age of ten;
    As he took leave from there,
    He knew where he had been.

    It was at that dear place
    He learned to read and write;
    And at his mother's knee,
    He gained his Christian sight.

    In his large family,
    Children numbered nineteen;
    Anytime at the Manse,
    Some children could be seen.

    His father was a priest,
    His mother was a saint;
    In all his years with them,
    He never learned "I can't."

    When he was only five,
    He could recite God's Word;
    It was the key language
    Of all that he had heard.

    His early school was home—
    His mother taught for free;

From her firm gentle way,
He knew what he could be.

Each child had his own time
With Susanna each week;
For John it was Thursday
He learned God's will to seek.

His mother strictly taught
Extinction of self-will;
To all of her children—
It was part of the drill.

Authoritarian
Was she with loving care—
Her children were her life;
The likes of her were rare.

A bond was there from birth
Throughout his many years;
John valued her great worth
And thought of her with tears.

John grew up in hard times—
All children had a chore;
Food was often scarce,
And hand-me-downs they wore.

Samuel had to garden
To keep them out of debt;
And that with his preaching
All bills were still not met.

His father went to jail
And stayed for many days—
A severe punishment
For his payment delays.

Confirmed by Bishop Wake
When he was only nine,
Wesley never forgot
His heritage, the vine.

The vine to him, the church,
Made him a branch alive;
Staying attached he knew
He would more than survive.

At his home in Epworth,
These younger years were yeast;
On them in later years,
His soul would often feast.

ALDERSGATE

There was a state of mind
In which he wished to dwell
And find his soul at peace
And all his actions well.

He went to Aldersgate,
Where friends had come for prayer;
He listened with his soul,
And something happened there.

His heart was strangely warmed—
God gave that state of mind
For which he sought so long,
And few can seldom find.

He felt that God forgave
Even his sins that night—
Bathing his soul in love
And drying it with light.

Assurance gained that night,
He knew he had the power
To meet his Lord's challenge
In any place or hour.

His zeal never slowed down—
He was forever bold;
But now it was so warm
Whereas it had been cold.

The Aldersgate event
Altered his state in life;
It set his soul at ease
Where once there had been strife.

HYMNS BASED ON WESLEY'S THEOLOGY AND LIFE

*All three of these hymns can be sung to the Azmon tune we use to
sing "O For a Thousand Tongues to Sing."*

THE LOVE THAT BROUGHT
THE CHRIST TO EARTH

The love that brought the Christ to earth
Still works to make him known,
And love reveals our sacred worth
When we become his own.

Love melts the hardness of our hearts
And gives us peace within.
Love puts together broken parts
And makes us whole again.

It binds together faith and deed
And makes our life complete.
This love in Christ will meet our need
And all our sins delete.

We love because God first loved us
In Christ of Galilee.
We share this love and what it does
To set his children free.

Across the world we take this news
Of what God does for all,
And even to those who refuse
Love will not build a wall.

LET US RECALL

Let us recall our heritage
And praise our Savior's name.
Our God has blessed us through the years.
His love remains the same.

Our strangely warmed and contrite hearts
No one can take away.
We know this from our heritage
And this we feel today.

Our church is built on Christ the rock
And it will always stand
As beacon light to those on sea
And all who walk the land.

Our church is guided by God's Word.
We study it with care
And in our prayers of every day
God comes to us to share.

Our church is strong because of Christ
And all who follow Him.
We strive each day to do His will.
Christ is our diadem.

Our parish is the world we claim
And it will always be.
The Great Commission is for us
Until eternity.

God sends us forth to share Good News.
We follow His command.
We never count the cost to us
When led by His own hand.

The Holy Scripture is our guide
To what we do believe.
We search its pages prayerfully
And wisdom we receive.

If things aren't clear in Holy writ,
Tradition is our guide.
The history of the church's thoughts
Helps us our faith decide.

Experience is valued much
When we are forming creeds.
Through it we know the living Christ
Who comes to meet our needs.

The mind that God has given us
We seek to use each day;
And reasoning in prayerful thought
Confirms the Christian way.

On this foundation we will build
Our faith in God who cares
For all His children of the earth
With whom He daily shares.

"The Holy Scripture Is Our Guide" hymn stresses the four-fold foun-
dation of our Methodist beliefs.

52